Written by Amelia Shearer
Illustrated by Kathryn Marlin

For manufacturing information regarding this product, please call 1-800-323-9400.

ISBN 978-1-4143-9481-7

Printed in the United States of America

21	20	19	18	
7	6	5	4	3

Tyndale House Publishers, Inc.
Carol Stream, Illinois

In spring I hear God's baby birds.

I smell God's fresh new flowers.

"Blossoms appear through all the land. The time has come to sing." *Song of Songs 2:12*

I hear the patter of God's rain.
He sends down helpful showers!

Spring shows me God is great!

I feel God's summer
heat outside.

His sun shines warm
and bright.

"The sun rises at one end of the sky,
and it follows its path to the other end.
Nothing hides from its heat." *Psalm 19:6*

I see God's many fireflies
and all his stars at night.

Summer shows me
God is great!

I see God's red and orange leaves.

I feel God's fall wind blow.

I taste a carrot from God's ground.
God made that carrot grow!

Fall shows me God is great!

In winter I feel cold snowflakes.

Each one God did create!

Winter, spring, summer, and fall—
seasons show me God is great!

"The heavens tell the glory of God. And the skies announce what his hands have made." *Psalm 19:1*